My House Shall Be a
House of Prayer

Compiled and Edited By Jonathan L. Graf and Lani C. Hinkle

A *Pray!* Magazine Book

Pray! Books • P.O. Box 35004 • Colorado Springs, Colorado 80935 • www.praymag.com

Contents

INTRODUCTION   4
My House Shall Be a House of Prayer

ONE: POWER HOUSE   7
How Prayer Can Saturate the Life of Your Church
Plus . . . "A Church That Prays"   9

TWO: FIRM FOUNDATIONS   13
A Blueprint for Building a House of Prayer
Plus . . . "Setting Up a Prayer Room"   16
Plus . . . "Shielding Pastors in Prayer"   18

THREE: WHO WILL HELP ME BUILD IT?   22
Pastor and Prayer Leader Working Together
Plus . . . "Prayer Leader Responsibilities"   27
Plus . . . "Developing a Prayer Strategy   28
for Your Church"
Plus . . . "Linking the Prayer Strategy with the Mission   30
of the Church"

FOUR: PRAYERLESS LEADERS = PRAYERLESS CHURCH   32
Three Steps to Get Your Leaders Praying

FIVE: BECOMING A PRAYING PASTOR   35
The first step: being honest with yourself.
Plus . . . "The Pastor as Prayer Leader"   39

SIX: WHAT DOES SCRIPTURE SAY?   41
A Bible Study for Church Leadership
About the Authors   45
What Is NALCPL?   47
What Is Pray!?   48

Introduction

My House Shall Be a House of Prayer

By Jonathan Graf

These days we love to think fondly of what Jesus said about His house being a house of prayer. Most of us would like to think, or simply assume, that our church is a house of prayer because it's a church that prays. But is it really a house of prayer? What did Jesus mean by that? What does a praying church look like?

If we are willing to admit that our church is not a house of prayer, how do we get there? What can I as a pastor, an intercessor, or a novice pray-er do to improve the prayer level at my church?

While the articles in this book do not give you a specific method for analyzing your church, each provides insights into what a house of prayer looks like and some suggestions on how to get there. As you read, think: *Is my church like this? Is our prayer emphasis this developed?* These kinds of questions will help you get a clearer picture.

When I consider the typical prayer levels in various churches, I see most fitting into one of three models. The diagram on page 5, based upon a concept developed by prayer leader Cheryl Sacks, best portrays the three models.

Diagram Explanation:

Church A is a church that hardly recognizes the importance of prayer to its ministry. It may give lip service to it by opening meetings in prayer, having a pastoral prayer in the worship service, and holding special prayer meetings from time to time for important issues. Prayer, however, is largely outside of the ministry. There may even be a few people praying for the church and its ministries, but they are not specifically given requests and are not recognized as a ministry of the church.

Church B recognizes that prayer is important. It wants to see things prayed for and wants to provide die-hard intercessors with a place to plug in. It recognizes prayer as a ministry of the church, much like youth or music. People who have an inner burden for prayer are involved, but not many others.

Church C believes that nothing lasting will happen apart from prayer. It believes that prayer needs to permeate every ministry of the church. Every ministry must be prayed for, and prayer must be a significant part of each ministry. Virtually everyone in the church is involved in prayer.

A.
Prayerless Church

Prayer · Youth Ministry · Elders · Small Groups · Outreach Ministry · Adult Ministry · Children's Ministry · Music Ministry

B.
Prayer Ministry Church

Youth Ministry · Elders · Small Groups · Adult Ministries · Music Ministry · Outreach Ministry · Prayer Ministry · Children's Ministry

C.
House of Prayer Church

Youth Ministry · Elders · Small Groups · Music Ministry · Prayer · Outreach Ministry · Children's Ministry · Adult Ministries

© 2000 by Cheryl Sacks

Perhaps you recognize your church somewhere in these diagrams. And no matter where you find it, there's hope in the pages that follow.

If your church is like A, then you need a radical paradigm shift. Your starting point is simply to pray that God would begin to bring about such a shift. As you read these articles, turn your dreams for what could be into prayer itself. Don't pray critically, but pray blessing on your church! Pray for a "grace of prayer" to fall upon your congregation.

If you see your church as B, you are well on your way. Praise God for what He is bringing about, and ask Him to take you further. You will see some very practical ideas in this issue. Begin to implement those that God seems to be leading you toward.

If you see your church in C, praise God! But don't rest. Keep seeking God to take your church deeper.

As I travel around the country, I am excited by what I see God doing in churches. He's giving congregations a continually increasing hunger for prayer! He can do it in your church, too. Perhaps He'll even continue the process as you read this book.

Power House

How Prayer Can Saturate the Life of Your Church

By Glen Martin and Dian Ginter

The year is 1971. Belmont Church of Nashville, Tennessee, is dying. It has about 60 members, no pastor, and is located in a transitional neighborhood. By all church growth principles, it is doomed. There is much talk about closing down. The situation seems hopeless, but God has other plans.

He brings to the church Pastor Don Finto, a man of vision for renewal, a man open to prayer. Because Finto transferred from a local Nashville church, the small group of about 12 who had been meeting with him regularly decided to transfer with him to Belmont. Prayer becomes the undergirding for everything at Belmont. This foundation, along with a close adherence to the Word and listening to the Spirit's direction, is credited for the 3,500 who worship there today.

Prayer saturates Belmont. Every weekday, members gather there at 5 a.m. to pray for one hour (or more) for personal and church concerns. Staff and leaders pray together weekly. The church offers a variety of other prayer opportunities: prayer cells, a weekly intercession group for children, women who pray for their families and husbands, a group that intercedes for Israel, prayer during Sunday school and church services, and missions prayer groups, to name just a few.

The church frequently calls special prayer meetings for specific causes and concerns in the congregation. It teaches often on the subject of prayer, including an annual prayer conference with an outside speaker.

Belmont has needed persistence to resist the enemy's attempts to discourage them from prayer; but the rewards have been many as they have pushed through the roadblocks.

Aldersgate United Methodist Church

A quarter of a million dollars in debt and only eight members! In 1979, this is what Terry Teykl faced when he accepted the pastoral call to the newly planted Aldersgate United Methodist Church in College Station, Texas. Not the ideal scenario for building a congregation into the more than 1,000 that attended weekly by 1993. Teykl confesses, "It was out of desperation that I first began to be really serious about prayer."

From that beginning, the Lord positioned prayer at the heart of the church. Like Belmont, it offers many places and ways for its people to be involved in prayer. Aldersgate also offers prayer at the altar for those who come forward at every service; prayer cover for the staff; a prayer room in which members commit to an hour a week to pray for the church, their schools, government, etc.; a monthly updated prayer list of members and visitors; "Aaronites," who have covenanted to pray one hour a day after being trained by the pastor; weekend prayer vigils; prayer seminars; and prayer that the city will be taken back for God. These prayer opportunities did not come into existence overnight. But, through the years, they have expanded beyond the "basics" of praying for the survival of the church and the needs of its members to praying for what lies outside its doors as well.

Teykl sums up their success: "We've learned what Jesus meant when He said, 'My Father's house shall be a house of prayer.' As we've organized prayer, the Holy Spirit has blessed our church in more ways than we can number; but especially, people have come to Christ and lives have been transformed. Any difficulties or setbacks in mobilizing the church to pray are well worth it to see the Holy Spirit bring people to

A CHURCH THAT PRAYS:	A CHURCH DEVOTED TO PRAYER:
1. Prays about what it does.	1. Does things by prayer.
2. Fits prayer in.	2. Gives prayer priority.
3. Prays when there are problems.	3. Prays when there are opportunities.
4. Announces a special time of prayer—some in the church show up.	4. Announces a special time of prayer—the entire church shows up.
5. Asks God to bless what it is doing.	5. Asks God to enable it to do what He is blessing.
6. Is frustrated by financial shortfall—backs down from projects.	6. Is challenged by financial shortfall—calls for fasting, prayer, and faith.
7. Is tired, weary, stressed out.	7. Mounts up with wings like eagles, runs and doesn't grow weary, walks and does not faint.
8. Does things within its means.	8. Does things beyond its means.
9. Sees its members as its parish.	9. Sees the world as its parish.
10. Is involved in the work of man.	10. Is involved in the work of God.
	—Fred A. Hartley III

Christ. For the sake of the kingdom of God, churches need to be on this cutting edge of praying the price."

Belmont and Aldersgate are not isolated examples. Similar accounts are being heard across the United States—accounts of churches that have placed prayer strategically at the heart of their ministry, with significant, even overwhelming, impact.

A powerful house of prayer is a church that understands that prayer acts as an oil upon it. Prayer will maximize all of its ministries; it will maintain a smooth-running operation. Prayer acts as a shield against the enemy's attacks on ministries and relationships.

There is a distinct difference between a church that has a prayer ministry and a church that is a house of prayer. A prayer ministry involves only a portion of the congregation—usually those with the greatest burden for prayer. This ministry may take the form of missionary prayer circles, an open Wednesday night prayer meeting, men's/women's/youth's prayer meetings, a prayer room, an intercessory team, prayer ministry before/during/after the church service, or a prayer chain. In such cases, prayer will be done by some but not all of the membership. It will be one of the important ministries of the church, like evangelism or choir.

While a prayer ministry is not a house of prayer, it is nevertheless important, because it can lay the foundation for becoming a house of prayer. Once a church acknowledges the strategic importance of prayer as a ministry, God can build on that to bring it to the next level.

In a powerful house of prayer, prayer will be foundational to and saturate every aspect of its individual and corporate life. Significant prayer will be top priority at every gathering, whatever its purpose. Prayer will be taught from the pulpit, in Sunday school classes, and in small groups. People will go to prayer first when they face a problem. Every member of the congregation will be involved to some degree.

Mindset is important. A church may have a prayer ministry, but a mentality that prevents it from taking the next step. In the ideal scenario, a church will first develop a strategic prayer ministry as a necessary and appropriate step. Then, when everyone is being encouraged to participate in one form or another, the church is on its way toward becoming a powerful house of prayer.

House of Prayer Characteristics

There are nine elements common to churches that are houses of prayer.

1. Prayer is visible from the pulpit. The church believes in prayer as a change agent and reaffirms it as a solution every Sunday. Preaching in the church will show how prayer is a vital attribute of biblical character and shines the way through personal struggles and trials. Writing to Timothy about essential leadership qualities, Paul says, "I urge, then, *first of all*, that requests, prayers, intercession and thanksgiving be made for everyone" (1 Tim. 2:1, *emphasis added*).

Prayer will be a key, not a suggestion at the end of a sermon. The congregation will appreciate the importance of prayer in everything they do because they've heard repeatedly how it has been an integral part of the lives of Jesus, biblical characters, and their pastor.

2. Prayer saturates every aspect of the service. Members have prayed throughout the week for the Sunday services and activities; several pray with the pastor before he speaks, and they pray during the service; people are available after the service to pray with anyone who desires it.

3. The leadership is committed to prayer. The leadership, staff, and key lay leaders have a burden for prayer and sense of expectancy from it. They are convinced of its effectiveness. It is a way of life for them, and they devote significant periods of time to developing it in their personal lives.

4. Prayer is an agenda item. Every group meeting—from leadership meetings and Sunday school classes to the least important board or committee meeting—will spend time praying. In addition to significant prayer at the beginning of meetings, they will stop and seek the Lord's face for wisdom, guidance, and oneness of mind when difficulties arise.

5. Prayer is part of Christian education. Periodically, Sunday school classes and/or small groups will do teaching series on prayer (in addition to their regular prayer commitments). They'll make learning about prayer a priority and they'll strive to make it meaningful for all.

6. The pastor has a strong prayer covering. Church leadership will receive unfailing prayer support for several reasons. First, leaders are prime targets for attack. Satan seems to watch for the best time— often landing blows right after a significant victory or when the leader is tired. Second, even the most godly leaders have weaknesses and cannot win the battle alone. Third, the people need to see and imitate leaders praying and being prayed for.

Prayer teams should pray daily for the pastor; for and during both morning and evening worship services; for the physical, emotional, intellectual, and spiritual life of their shepherd and his family; for protection over him, his family, possessions, and reputation.

7. Prayer is the first step, not the last resort. Groups of people pray spontaneously together about problems and interests. Prayer is always the first step in finding a solution. Thus, pray-ers are available after services for those who have specific needs. A prayer room may be designated for those who desire confidentiality or need a longer prayer time.

8. Intercession is an integral part of the church life. A variety of times and places are available for people to gather for prayer—in the early morning, during lunch, or after work; at church, in homes, or at a restaurant over a meal; at a business, or with other business people in the area. A strong and efficient prayer chain is in place to serve the congregation's emergency needs, as well as a mechanism whereby people can share the answers to those requests. Prayer looks not only inward at the church, but will be a dynamic, powerful, and tangible means of influencing the city, state, government, and world.

9. The church has a recognized prayer leader other than the senior pastor. As a church becomes excited about prayer and its developing prayer skills, it will seek more direction. A director of prayer (either paid staff or lay leader) will develop ministries and annual seminars that impact the local body and create a greater sense of awareness of the need for prayer. The church that is increasing its outreach to the community will most likely have a prayer director that is paid staff.

It is no simple task to become a powerful house of prayer. Satan will fight every step of the way. If prayer is going to pervade the church of the 21st century and communicate the gospel to our world, however, innovation and perseverance must be employed. Jesus spoke of the gospel as "new wine" that could not be contained in "old wineskins." So break the traditional mold for prayer in your church. Get "radical" and aim precisely at what our Lord has set before us. Strive to become a powerful house of prayer that brings God's people into alignment with His principles and spreads the truth for His glory.

This article is adapted from *Power House: A Step-By-Step Guide to Building a Church That Prays*
© 1994 Broadman & Holman Publishers. Used by Permission.

Firm Foundations

A Blueprint for Building a House of Prayer

By Wes Tullis

The first administrative decision made by the apostles was to "give [their] attention to prayer and the ministry of the word" (Acts 6:4). This first example of local church prayer had dramatic results: "The word of God spread" (Acts 6:7).

When Jesus rode triumphantly into Jerusalem, He painted a picture of how God would bring His full authority and reign to earth when He said, "My house will be a house of prayer for all nations" (Mk. 11:17).

While becoming a "house of prayer" is modeled and mandated in Scripture, getting there is not an instantaneous act in today's church. God's people must first be awakened to the importance of prayer; then they need to be equipped in prayer; then they can be released for strategic involvement in prayer. The process of establishing a full-orbed prayer focus within a local church can take three to five years. It's critical to begin with realistic time-frame expectations. Too many have begun as positive change-agents in their churches only to give up after a year or two, disgruntled and bitter toward their churches and leadership teams.

The following priorities can help you begin with a firm foundation as you initiate the process of prayer mobilization in your church:

Priority 1: Select a Prayer Leader

While the senior pastor is key to moving a church toward becoming a house of prayer (it will not happen unless he is 100 percent behind it and driving the changes), the task is too enormous for him to facilitate the nitty-gritty operations. A lay person with a heart for prayer and, perhaps, a gift of administration should be selected by the senior pastor. This person will work closely with the leadership team as the ministry of prayer develops.

Priority 2: Meet with Church Leadership

Before any changes are made, it is important that all church leaders understand the heart, vision, and concerns of the pastor(s) and prayer leader. Keep in mind that all prayer ministries exist to strengthen the life and mission of the local church. Everything you initiate in the prayer ministry should tie in to the church's mission and goals.

Priority 3: Fast and Pray with a Team

Again, before making any changes, find a team of like-minded brothers and sisters who will meet consistently (at least once a week) for a period of time (30 to 90 days) to soak the entire process with fasting and prayer.

Ask the Lord for personal cleansing and to expose any areas of your lives that violate honesty in His presence or hinder humility, holiness, and hunger for Him. This prayer period is the most important time in the development of your prayer strategies. Just as the foundation work is the most important part of building construction (yet the least visible), so it is here. Know that you are sowing healthy spiritual seeds, and you will reap a harvest.

Priority 4: Publicly Introduce and Commission the Local Church Prayer Leader

The senior pastor should publicly commission the person who will serve as the local church prayer leader. We suggest that the church leadership pray over and commission this person during the main church services. The senior pastor plays an indispensable role in the success of the prayer ministry. His support, endorsement, and involvement at pivotal times are vital if the entire church is to understand this is not a peripheral effort, but the core of the life of the fellowship.

Priority 5: Establish Pillars of Prayer

It's critical to establish the pillars on which the ministry will rest. We recommend these "Four Pillars of Prayer," used by churches that have successfully become houses of prayer:
• Establish a strategic plan of prayer for your church
• Establish a prayer shield for leadership
• Establish a prayer room
• Establish a prayer evangelism focus (a plan for how you will pray for the lost outside your walls).

Priority 6: Connect with the Body of Christ

Don't try to do everything alone. Network with other church prayer leaders in your city and around the nation. Meet together to compare notes and encourage each other. To find other local leaders, simply call some churches in your community, explain what you want to do, and ask if they have a recognized prayer leader you could make contact with. If your city already has some form of church networking, start there.

I also highly recommend that you join a network, such as the National Association of Local Church Prayer Leaders (NALCPL). A few denominations, such as the Southern Baptists and the Christian Church (Harvest Prayer Resource Network), also have established networks of prayer leaders.

Ultimately, all of our efforts toward prayer mobilization in the church should be geared to help believers experience vibrancy. A house of prayer provides opportunities for members to grow (1) in their personal times with the Lord; (2) in their prayer times with spouses and children; (3) in small groups/cell groups of prayer and ministry that are strongly connected to the life and mission of the local church; and (4) in personal and corporate times of prayer for revival, transformation of the community, and completion of the Great Commission. Any attempts at prayer mobilization will be ineffective unless these foundational goals are in place. But when they are clearly articulated and are serving to draw church members into stronger communion with the Lord each day, then you have a church that is becoming a house of prayer.

Setting Up a Prayer Room

By Terry Teykl

One of the core needs of any praying church is a prayer room. This physical space, set aside for the sole purpose of prayer, serves as a command center for the prayer ministry, gives the prayer ministry a presence in the church, and allows prayer activities to flourish without interference or distraction. The following guidelines are designed to help you get started:

1. Decide on a location. Your imagination is the limit—find a classroom, an unused office, a storage room, a portable building, the basement. What the original space looks like is not important. Your primary considerations should be accessibility, security, visibility, and size. You don't have to limit your search to the church facility. Many prayer rooms are being set up in public places, some through the cooperative efforts of several churches who share the expenses and upkeep. In Douglasville, Georgia, there is a prayer room in an abandoned downtown courthouse; in Tehachapi, California, there is a prayer place in the crisis pregnancy center. In Spring, Texas, there's one in a bank building office.

2. Make a list of prayer stations needed. (A prayer station is a section of the room that focuses on one thing: missions, schools, etc.)

Several factors will influence the content and personality of your prayer room—visions and ministries of sponsoring churches, outreach opportunities, location, needs of the community. Consider the special needs of those who might come to pray (children or the elderly, for example) as well as postures that might be used in prayer (standing, kneeling, sitting, or lying). Visiting other prayer rooms or inquiring about them by phone will probably stir up more ideas than you know what to do with. Listen to the Holy Spirit for specific direction.

The key to prayer stations is information. With so much to pray about, intercessors can become overwhelmed. Well-organized prayer stations with specific information can help. Each station should focus on one primary area, and include many possible sub categories. Lists of names, specific needs, testimonies, maps, current local, state, national, and global issues—all this information enables intercessors to pray with more precision and passion.

3. Set a budget and make a shopping list. Make the most of whatever resources you have to create a place that is inviting, inspiring, and well-ordered. You are likely to need tables, chairs, lamps, pillows, plants, boxes, card files, notebooks, maps, pictures, pencils, and a tape or CD player. Attention to detail will ensure that your prayer room is functional and comfortable.

4. Think it through. For each station, ask practical questions such as, "How will prayer requests be gathered and organized? Who will update the information and how often? What kinds of prayer guides or helps might be useful? When possible, provide actual names and places to be targeted in prayer, such as schools, government officials, gangs, and other churches. Such specifics motivate intercessors and make it easier to provide feedback and answers to prayer.

5. Be creative. Whatever your specific choices, set up the new prayer place with enthusiasm and expectation. This is the beginning of a dynamic influence in your church or community.

Shielding Pastors in Prayer

By Mell Winger

When I was a pastor years ago, I learned firsthand about the defensive power of having people behind the scenes praying for me—of having a "prayer shield." I had been teaching a class on cults and world religions. Sadly, I found myself spending more time reading the twisted thoughts of the cultist than God's Word. One morning, I arose at 4 a.m. to cram in some "cult studies" before teaching my class.

After about an hour of reading false doctrine, I sensed a growing darkness, which clouded my thoughts. Oppression engulfed me, and I sank into depression and doubt. I immediately fell to my knees and began to cry out to God for mercy. In just moments, the heaviness lifted and my thoughts were clear.

Four hours later, as I arrived to teach my class, a woman who regularly prayed for me rushed up and greeted me with, "What was happening to you at 5 a.m.?" I jokingly blurted out, "Oh, not much. I just felt like I was snapping!" She told me how the Lord awakened her at 5 a.m. and said, "Pray for Mell right now!" She had battled intensely for me in prayer. Tears of awe and gratitude welled up within me as I realized that this explained why the oppression over me had lifted so quickly: An interceding believer had entered into my struggle!

Just last year, while I was a missionary in Guatemala, I had an experience that vividly illustrated the offensive strength of the prayer shield.

An attorney had detained documents that proved I had legally purchased my van. For months I drove the van without a proper title. Each time I passed a policeman, the thought of being thrown into a foreign jail produced a churning in my stomach. Eventually, I discovered that the attorney had taken the exorbitant fees I paid him for securing my van title and spent the money on himself.

For seven months, I desperately enlisted others to help. I prayed. I plotted. I whined. All was futile. Finally, I resorted to notifying the 50 plus believers in my prayer shield to pray for this situation. Within two weeks I had my title and a refund of $400! (Incidentally, the week after my title finally arrived I was stopped three times by police to check my title and license!)

Prayer shields for Christian leaders are as old as the New Testament. The apostle Paul underscored the necessity of interceding for spiritual leaders in eight places throughout his letters (2 Cor. 1:11, Eph. 6:18-19, Phil. 1:19, Col. 4:2-4, 1 Thess. 5:25, 2 Thess. 3:1-2, Phlm. 22).

Note the passionate words Paul wrote to the Roman believers: "Stand behind me in earnest prayer to God on my behalf" (Ro. 15:30, *Phillips*). Most pastors and Christian leaders who have faced ministry pressures and spiritual struggles have uttered this same plea. Today, many pastors and leaders are experiencing the power of having a prayer shield. They are not ashamed to ask for prayer.

Whether you are an intercessor or a pastor, one of the most important things you can do as you seek to make your church a house of prayer is to develop a prayer shield for pastors and leaders in your church. But where should you begin?

Building a Pastor's Prayer Shield

When building a prayer shield, it helps to think in terms of three sequential phases: designing, sustaining, and expanding.

1. Design Phase

In this initial phase there are three areas to determine: selecting and forming the prayer team, defining the relationship and boundaries, and establishing the channels of communication.

Selecting the prayer team. The best place to begin in selecting the members for your shield is with prayer. Remember that Jesus spent the night in prayer before He selected the 12 disciples. The Lord will guide you in this process.

Here are essential qualities for your prayer partners:
1) A heart for prayer.
2) A heart for the pastor, his family, and ministry.
3) A humble, consistent Christian character.
4) An ability to respect confidential information.
5) Faithfulness in the local church.

In most cases, it is wise to first select a person to oversee the prayer shield. This person can handle the details and facilitate the communication flow between the prayer partners and the pastor. This person should possess all of the qualities above, plus organizational gifts and a grasp of basic prayer principles.

Defining the boundaries. On occasion the pastor's accessibility is critical to the success of the prayer shield, but this can become very time consuming. Therefore boundaries should be established up front as to the amount time the pastor, as the leader, is accessible to his prayer partners. Establishing the boundaries early can preclude an unhealthy dependency developing between the leader and the prayers. It is wise to determine that a male pastor will not meet alone with the opposite sex to discuss prayer needs.

Establishing the channels of communication. Consistent communication is critical for an effective prayer covering. This can generally be through e-mails and letters or through phone calls for emergency needs. Someone must be responsible for maintaining the communication flow.

It is helpful to establish some general guidelines for prayer in addition to your personal prayer needs. For example, send out lists of Bible verses for the team to pray over you. Colossians 1:9-14 and Eph. 1:17-23 are fabulous verses. Develop prayer targets for each day of the week or each week.

2. Sustaining Phase

People who pray for pastors and leaders need to be:

Connected. A sense of connectedness is essential for the success of a prayer shield. Praying believers want to give their time to something worthwhile. Someone has noted, "People stay involved when they stay informed." Providing important details of the pastor's life and ministry helps to keep those praying involved.

Updated. Nothing ignites and sustains prayer quite like answers to prayer. Those who pray for leaders need to hear encouraging reports of answers to their intercession.

Appreciated. If prayer partners do not feel appreciated, eventually many will gravitate toward new prayer assignments. Those committing to pray for a leader often stay up late praying, spend time fasting, and postpone their own personal prayer needs for the sake of the leader. It is only common courtesy to acknowledge this sacrifice. Simple "thank you" notes are an easy beginning point.

3. Expanding Phase

All prayer shields seem to have a built-in attrition. There will be times when more intercessors will need to be added to the prayer shield because people have dropped out. At some point, having partners reenlist for another commitment period is helpful. Periodically recruit new people. Fresh troops will add a renewed dimension of strength to the shield. How do you know when to add more pray-ers? When you are consistently overwhelmed by the battles, you should consider reinforcements.

Prayer shields require input and regular maintenance like most valuable endeavors in life. The payoff is undoubtedly worth the effort. Ask anyone in ministry who has experienced the blessing of prayer support. More than likely, they would never consider ministering again without this "behind the scenes" team of warriors.

CHAPTER THREE

Who Will Help Me Build It?

Pastor and Prayer Leader Working Together

By Cheryl Sacks

*I*t was Sunday morning and the 2,500-seat auditorium was filled to near capacity. It was Focus on the Family's Clergy Appreciation Sunday, and Julie Touvell, the prayer leader at The Valley Cathedral, realized this was a great opportunity to launch the new adopt-a-pastor-in-prayer initiative.

The congregation was visibly surprised that morning when their pastor came to the platform. Instead of receiving expensive gifts of appreciation, he bore upon his chest a large black and white target with a red bull's eye.

"We are in a real battle," Julie told the congregation as she explained the critical need to pray for the pastor and church leaders. "In spiritual warfare, the church is the target, and the pastor is the bull's eye!"

"Pastors are vulnerable when they stand alone," she said. Then, as intercessors encircled the pastor, she continued, "See, the target is no longer visible. When we stand with our pastor in prayer, he is shielded from the enemy."

Julie then invited church members to choose one of the staff pastors to adopt in prayer for the next three months. "The best gift we can give our pastor and church leaders," she said, "is the gift of prayer."

Following the service, people flooded to the information center to sign up. There they found pictures of the church's 12 staff pastors and an enthusiastic volunteer to assist those who were willing to participate. To the pastors' and Julie's delight, 400 people adopted a pastor in prayer that day!

The Church Prayer Leader

In churches all across America, prayer leaders like Julie are assisting their pastors in mobilizing their church to pray successfully. Just as every other ministry in the church has a leader, so the prayer ministry needs a designated person to coordinate prayer. Too often we think prayer will happen on its own. If we are to be a praying church, however, we must be intentional about mobilizing prayer. The selection of a church prayer leader is foundational to this process.

Prayer leaders ensure that intercession is raised up not only for pastors, but also for children, youth, marriages, missions, and more. Their role is to see that prayer is integrated into the total life of the church.

The prayer leader should be a member of the church who organizes, schedules, and provides general leadership for all the church's prayer activities. Together with the pastor, the prayer leader gives energy and direction to the church's prayer organization.

The prayer leader's title may vary from prayer coordinator or ministry director to pastor of prayer. The position may be filled by a full- or part-time paid staff member or volunteer.

Because the position of prayer leader is new to many churches, pastors frequently ask the question, "How do I select the right person?" The most common mistake made by pastors when selecting a prayer leader is choosing a member of the congregation with the greatest gifting and desire to pray. This may not always be the best person for the job. Unless the prayer leader also has administrative gifts and the ability to mobilize others to pray, the ministry may never get off the ground.

Characteristics of a Successful Prayer Leader:
- A strong personal prayer life, as well as gifts to lead, organize, and mobilize.

- Commitment to the pastor and to the vision and purpose of the church.
- Proven spiritual maturity, a good reputation in the congregation, and the confidence of the church leadership.
- The ability to lead or learn to lead small group and corporate prayer.
- Ease in speaking before people.
- The desire and ability to develop and work with a prayer team.
- Time to coordinate the activities of the prayer ministry, and attend key prayer events in the church and community.
- A teachable spirit, with the time and desire to become further trained in this ministry.

The Pastor/Prayer Leader Relationship

I have been training and networking some 400 church prayer leaders throughout Arizona for the past several years. Frequently, I ask prayer leaders and their pastors to share their greatest frustrations in working together.

Prayer leaders inevitably share their need for more pastoral support. They say it is disheartening to work alongside a pastor who says prayer is a priority—when in reality the pastor is too busy to offer time and resources to prayer events and the prayer ministry.

Pastors talk about feeling pressured by expectations in the face of already-packed schedules and feeling as though they are tagged as "unspiritual" by prayer leaders and intercessors. They say the overall well-being of the church is damaged when prayer leaders exhibit an attitude of superiority because of their dedication to prayer. Instead of feeling supported and blessed by the prayer leader and prayer ministry, the pastor often feels put down or alienated.

The success of any prayer ministry is dependent upon the positive working relationship between the pastor and church prayer leader. It is therefore imperative that pastors and prayer leaders show mutual support for one another. To do this, communication lines need to be kept open and expectations clearly defined.

Practical Tips for Pastors:

- The first ingredient in a praying church begins with three simple words: a praying pastor. No amount of energy or vision on the part of the prayer leader can take the place of your personal prayer life.
- Give the prayer leader the same level of respect as you do your worship leader, youth pastor, or Christian education director.
- Publicly affirm and recognize your prayer leader and his/her role in the church. This signals that prayer is a core value to the church, brings focus and intention to the prayer ministry, provides a way to recruit intercessors, and encourages greater prayer participation from the congregation.
- Develop a job description and clarify to whom the prayer leader will report.
- Encourage and assist your prayer leader in building a prayer team, developing a prayer strategy, and establishing a budget. (Prayer ministry takes manpower, planning, and money, just like any other ministry.)
- Set regular appointments with your prayer leader to pray with him/her and evaluate the progress of the ministry.
- Draw your prayer leader into the leadership circle of the church. This will ensure that prayer does not become an isolated ministry, but a part of the fabric of the church.
- Teach on and model prayer from the pulpit, and promote the many times and ways in which your church members can get involved in prayer. Remember, no matter who heads it, the senior pastor must visibly and solidly support the ministry of prayer.

Practical Tips for Prayer Leaders:

- Pray for your pastor and his/her family daily. Make mobilizing prayer for the pastor a top priority.
- Always speak well of your pastor, other ministry leaders, and their families. Do not entertain gossip. Avoid the hook of the enemy to draw you in with remarks such as, "Our pastor just isn't interested in prayer."
- Allow the pastor to lead the process, impart vision, and set the pace for prayer mobilization.

- Develop a prayer strategy that complements the vision of the pastor and supports the ministries in the church. Remember you will lead best by serving.
- Keep your pastor informed about what you are doing through meetings, memos, e-mails, and letters. Be sure to seek pastoral advice and endorsement before asking anyone to serve in a leadership role.
- Be patient with the process of becoming a praying church. Developing a comprehensive prayer strategy can take three to five years. Don't give up!

The House of Prayer

A gifted prayer leader can do much by coming alongside the pastor to build a successful prayer ministry. However, this is only the beginning. God's heart is after something more. His desire is that your congregation will be known as a house of prayer—a habitation for His presence and glory that transcends the walls of your church.

The goal is for prayer to saturate every aspect of the individual and corporate life of the church. In this stage, the entire congregation becomes consumed with a passion for intimacy with Christ that spills over into the entire community.

It is like the dream a prayer leader at Second Baptist Church in Boerne, Texas, shared with me: "All of a sudden it began to rain in the sanctuary. The people were rejoicing. They didn't seem to mind the rain at all! As the worship became sweeter and the prayer more fervent, the water kept getting higher and higher. Then someone opened the door and the water began to flow out of the church and into the street. It touched everything in its path—homes, other churches, people without Christ. And everywhere the water flowed, there was life."

I believe this dream is symbolic of what God is about to do with His houses of prayer. He is calling the church to a place of intimacy with Him. As we respond by inviting the presence of the Lord into our midst, we will see the power of God transform our churches, communities, and world.

I hear the Lord asking, "Who will help me build this house of prayer?" Is it you?

Prayer Leader Responsibilities

By Cheryl Sacks

The following job description for prayer leaders is a guideline. The pastor and prayer leader should determine what his or her exact responsibilities should be.

- Identify key people in the church who are willing to pray or serve in leadership of the prayer ministry and enlist their support.
- Establish a strategic prayer committee and serve as its chairperson. (The leadership responsibilities of the prayer ministry can be divided among the members of this committee.)
- Act as a liaison between the pastor and church leadership and the prayer committee.
- Assist the pastoral staff in raising up their personal prayer support teams.
- Co-labor with the prayer committee and church leadership to plan prayer for corporate services.
- Work with the pastor and prayer committee to develop a mission statement for the prayer ministry and a prayer strategy for the church.
- Aid the development of the prayer chain.
- Create a resource library on prayer.
- Enable Sunday school teachers and small group leaders by providing training, materials, and resources for their prayer curriculum.
- Plan and organize special prayer events in the church (i.e., prayer conferences, workshops, National Day of Prayer).
- Train and equip prayer leaders who can establish and lead small group prayer.
- Set up (with prayer committee and church leadership) a prayer room in the church.

- Create an information network that keeps everyone informed of prayer concerns.
- Serve as a liaison between your church and churches citywide to foster cooperative prayer efforts.
- Ensure that prayer is mobilized in and integrated into every ministry and department of the church.

Developing a Prayer Strategy for Your Church

By Gary Kinnaman and Cheryl Sacks

Of all the goals in the 50-page strategic plan for our large church, not one of them is "to pray." Intercessor, do I have your attention?

Well, we definitely have a heart and passion to pray! The pediment above one of the entry doors into our worship center reads, "My house shall be called a house of prayer." But "being a praying church" is not one of our official vision statements.

Why? Because prayer for prayer's sake is purposeless. However, the first of our 10 goals is "to worship God and cultivate our relationship with Him." Our goal isn't to pray, or even to have a prayer ministry. Our goal is to know God. That brings us to our knees. Fervent prayer and a prayer ministry are means to that chief end.

And to that end, Cheryl [Sacks] and I, along with other leaders, developed a strategic plan for mobilizing and sustaining prayer within our church. You need a strategic plan as well. Here are some suggestions as to where to start:

- The first thing to do is (you guessed it) PRAY! Ask the Lord to guide you in developing a strategy that will help your congregation become a praying church. Pray for the Lord to release a spirit of prayer upon your congregation and make your church a house of prayer.
- Start with a brainstorming session with your church leadership team.
- The prayer strategy should include a mission statement, core values,

goals, objectives, a timeline, and an organizational chart.

• Build your prayer strategy from the mission of the church. Although all churches are called to advance Christ's kingdom, each one will have a different way of fulfilling that mission. If your church doesn't have a clear mission statement with goals and objectives, this is one of the first things to pray for. Pray that your church will know where it's going and how to get there. Once your church develops overall goals and objectives, then the prayer ministry can come alongside with a strategy that supports every ministry of the church.

• Evaluate the present ministry of prayer. Find out what is already going on and then seek ways to strengthen existing prayer ministries.

• Build prayer into Christian education. To teach people to pray is to teach them to triumph. It is impossible to mobilize people to pray if they don't have a heart for prayer, if they don't believe they serve the God of the impossible, or if they don't know how to pray. If you are the pastor, preach and teach on prayer and encourage Sunday school teachers and small group leaders to do so as well.

• Make many times, places, and ways to pray. With the overload on most people's schedules today, we need to offer them a variety of prayer opportunities. Consider building prayer into existing ministries before adding additional meetings for prayer. Also remember that some people who would never attend a prayer meeting at church would pray at home if given the prayer requests.

• Pray over the weak and potentially vulnerable places in the church. Ask yourself "Where does the enemy come in time and time again?" Is it lack of finances, moral failures, backsliding youth, chronic illness, divorce or marital disunity, or even death? When the enemy comes in like a flood, mount a counterattack, calling upon the name of the Lord.

• Create a strategy for prayer mobilization. A great tip: enlist people to pray for the areas that are on their hearts. The best motivation to pray is love. Find out what people love and connect them with that area of prayer. Some members would love to pray for unreached people groups. Others would be privileged to pray with someone else for a wayward teenager or unsaved spouse.

- Always remember that the ultimate goal is not to develop a prayer ministry—it is to become a praying church. Some ministries in the church are vertical silos (such as the men's ministry, youth groups, or small groups). Other ministries, such as prayer, worship, and discipleship must run horizontally, touching each ministry in the church. It is important, therefore, that prayer is not isolated in one area or one group of the church. Rather, it should be at the heart of everything the church does.

Whatever you do as you develop a church prayer strategy, don't give up. There will be resistance from the enemy. If plans fail, don't be discouraged; be flexible. If you must, start over, but purpose to keep moving ahead. And most of all, keep on praying!

Linking the Prayer Strategy with the Mission of the Church

By Cheryl Sacks

The book of Acts offers a powerful model of the marriage of prayer and the mission of the church. As the saints prayed fervently, the church increased exponentially. Current statistics show that church leaders who are prayed for are more effective and ministry that is coupled with prayer is many times more fruitful. An effective prayer strategy should relate to the mission statement of the church (not be independent of it).

Although every church's mission statement is unique, most will include three components: WIN, BUILD, and SEND. A good mission plan will further break down into goals and objectives that translate into manageable tasks. These become the road map for developing and implementing your church's prayer strategy.

An example of this can be seen in the mission of Orangewood Nazarene Church in Phoenix, Arizona. Its mission statement reads: *We are a community of believers passionate about presenting Jesus and equipping people to become fully devoted followers of Jesus Christ.* One way the church will fulfill this mission is through its WIN (evangelism) goal of seeing every person within a one-mile radius of the church come to Christ. The question must then be asked, "How can the prayer strategy support this mission goal?"

The Orangewood prayer ministry developed a plan to mobilize the church family to prayerwalk the perimeter of the targeted neighborhood. It also ordered an ariel photograph of the one-mile radius and secured the names of every resident within that location. Intercessors pray for each person by name (and for a three-month period someone was in the prayer room 24-hours a day praying for the salvation of each household).

In addition to the overall mission statement, every ministry or department of the church will have its own individual mission and goals. For example, the prayer ministry will need to develop a plan to WIN (recruit) and BUILD (train) the church's intercessors then SEND (release) them into every ministry of the church. Holding a consultation with the leader of each ministry or department of the church can help you discover the best ways to support each ministry's mission in prayer.

When I talked with the youth pastor at Living Streams Church in Phoenix, Arizona, I found the church had a goal to BUILD (disciple) its youth to be living witnesses for Christ. To help accomplish this goal, we developed a prayer strategy whereby every youth in the church was adopted in prayer by an adult intercessor for an entire year. Every intercessor carried in his or her Bible a picture of the youth for whom he or she was praying. This was a daily reminder to pray that each young person would grow in the knowledge of Christ, be steadfast in his or her faith, not yielding to peer pressure, but sharing his or her faith boldly.

As you continue to follow the road map of your church's mission statement, the Holy Spirit will give you creative prayer strategies to support each church goal. Soon you'll discover that prayer is saturating every aspect of your church's WINNING, BUILDING, and SENDING strategy.

CHAPTER FOUR

Prayerless Leaders = Prayerless Church

Three Steps to Get Your Leaders Praying

By Dave Butts

Recently, when I visited the Brooklyn Tabernacle's Tuesday night prayer meeting (with more than 2,000 in attendance), it impressed me that the first three rows in the sanctuary were roped off. These rows were reserved for the leaders of the church. They were expected to be there—down front—and visible to the rest of the congregation. That was their place as leaders of prayer for the church.

Brooklyn Tabernacle understands that godly leaders need to step out by faith in the direction that God lays out before them, and the people of God will follow—especially in the area of prayer. The local church will not become a house of prayer until its *leaders become people of prayer.* When prayer has its proper place in the life of church leaders, it will move to a place of centrality in the rest of the church.

For many churches, one of the biggest roadblocks to increased prayer is the indifference of—or even opposition from—its leaders (elders, deacons, board members). Many leaders simply do not recognize the importance of prayer to the life of a church. While many churches are not ready to "expect" their leaders to display their support of prayer like the Brooklyn Tabernacle does, a pastor or prayer leader can do a number of things to encourage a change in attitude.

Teaching

Believe it or not, the concept of a prayer ministry is new to many leaders. They assume that Christians pray and that there will always be some degree of prayer within the church. But in order for leaders to understand the biblical view of the church as a house of prayer, teaching will be necessary. This instruction needs to be on two levels.

First of all, among the church leadership itself, there should be regular times of studying both the biblical concepts of a praying church as well as the practical contemporary issues of prayer ministry. Then, on a broader level, the entire congregation needs to be exposed to these concepts through sermons and Bible study times.

Practice

One of the most important steps for prayer ministry leadership is "just do it." Set a time that works for your leaders and get together regularly for prayer. If possible, include "regularly attends leadership prayer meetings" in the job description of your leadership positions.

When leaders pray together, it allows them to call the rest of the church to prayer with integrity, it unifies them in a vision for the church, and it gives them confidence to lead others in prayer.

What should church leaders pray for when they come together?

A spirit of prayer. One of the most powerful things that leaders can ask God is to pour out a spirit of prayer upon their congregation. This request assures that they are not looking at prayer as a program, but that they are completely dependent upon the Lord to transform His people. It never works to "guilt" people into praying; but God can pour out a burden for prayer upon them. Ask Him to do it!

Church members. When leaders commit to pray for the church on a regular basis, it can be a wonderful spiritual adventure. Gather names, divide them among your leaders, and begin to cover your congregation in prayer. It's an exciting way to demonstrate love and leadership!

Each other. Don't forget to pray for each other. Ministering to one another in prayer is a great way to build unity as a leadership team.

A great example of this is happening at the Brownsburg (Indiana)

Christian Church. The elders and pastor there made a decision to gather for prayer every Saturday morning. After doing that for a number of months, they began to invite the congregation to join them, either to pray or receive prayer. Last January, on Inauguration Day, more than 500 people joined them to pray for the new president. That dynamic hour of prayer continues to impact the church.

Vision

In most churches, at least if they are completely honest, becoming a house of prayer is not a typical vision. If your church is going to become a house of prayer, a clear vision must be developed and communicated. One way to develop that vision would be for church leaders to visit other churches that are functioning as houses of prayer (Brooklyn Tabernacle, for instance). Enrolling leaders in a College of Prayer program may also be a worthwhile experience. Visit the World Prayer Center in Colorado Springs, Colorado, or attend a National Association of Local Church Prayer Leaders conference. These kinds of experiences will stimulate new ways of looking at church prayer ministry.

Get Started

In the early church, virtually every church meeting was a prayer meeting. Leaders in the Jerusalem church understood that their God-given priorities were "prayer and the ministry of the Word" (Acts 6:4). Godly leaders came together in prayer to seek the face of God, to spend time with Him in prayer, and to allow the One who is Head of the body take leadership over His body. As this begins to happen within leadership structures of the local church today, congregations will begin to follow. Prayer will not be simply an add-on program in an already busy church—it will be the very center of its life.

The prayer movement that is under way in the world today is not the latest fad that will be replaced when some other new movement comes along. It is a *restoration of a lifestyle that the Lord has always expected us to live*. Godly, praying leaders are the key. It's time for them to step out in prayer and lead their congregations back to the power of God.

CHAPTER FIVE

Becoming a Praying Pastor

The first step: being honest with yourself.

By Steve Loopstra

I suppose my prayer life was not much different from many pastors. Certainly, I prayed for my church. But then I searched for programs that promised to grow it—remembering, of course, to ask God to bless those programs!

So you can imagine the depth of conviction I felt when God moved in my heart to write letters to the churches I had pastored, asking their forgiveness for being a "pastor who prayed," but not a "praying pastor." Perhaps the story of my journey will speak to others who are struggling with what it means to be a praying pastor.

Immersed in War and the Word

Before I came to Christ, I was well on my way to destruction through drugs, alcohol, and lifestyle choices. I was rescued through faith in Jesus Christ at the age of 19, while in the Air Force and on my way to Vietnam. A Christian servicemen's center gave me access to a host of wonderful resources by classic Christian writers, and I was soaked in scriptural truth through books by A. W. Tozer, Oswald Chambers, J. Oswald Sanders, A. B. Simpson, and others. As a baby Christian in a war-torn nation, I grew in faith through profound writings on the foundational principles of prayer and revival. It wasn't until some time later that I discovered that not every believer was grounded in those same truths and passions.

At a Bible conference in Bangkok, Thailand, I knew the Lord was calling me to serve Him. I followed the counsel of others and went on to Bible college and seminary. Those years of training taught me to love the Word of God even more. But then I began to experience a subtle change in my thinking and understanding. I slowly began to rely more on the skills I was learning, and less on my initial child-like reliance on hearing directly from the Father.

"Church in a Can" Approach

After graduation, I discovered that pastoring a church was a major challenge! I loved preaching and teaching the Word of God, but I soon learned that people expected more. They expected plans and programs and results. Not only did I feel those expectations from the people in my church, but also from leadership in the denomination. Ever so slowly, I began to look for help from programs and methods of church growth, evangelism, and discipleship.

I can look back now and see that I was, in some ways, looking for "church in a can" to help me be on the cutting edge of ministry. I would look for something that seemed to fit my congregation and myself, then go to the training and get the notebook. I would come back, present it to the board, and then pray that God would use it to build my church.

I really thought that was the way to do it, partly because it came so naturally, but also because it seemed to be the "culture." I saw other pastors doing the same thing; in fact, we would meet each other at conference after conference. Even my denominational leaders would promote this program or that seminar. It became the lifestyle.

Deep within me, however, I felt a growing dissatisfaction. I was getting tired of the endless parade of programs. I think my people were getting tired of them! They did them because I "believed" in them. But I didn't really believe in them; mostly, I was "hoping" in them to do the job.

The Root of Dissatisfaction

Thankfully, my heart began to change when I started attending pastors' prayer summits sponsored by our denomination. I discovered that the *dissatisfaction* I was feeling was, in reality, my *distance* from my heavenly Father. My prayer life deepened as I learned to view prayer as part of my love relationship with a God who was seeking me out. I later described it as "God romancing me back to Himself."

The lid finally came off for me at an annual denominational meeting. I was attending a sacred assembly of prayer, when the Lord spoke very directly to me: I had been a pastor who prayed, but not a praying pastor. The distinction was extremely clear to me. A praying pastor is one who knows how to spend time in the presence of the Father, seeking Him and hearing what His heart is for the church. A praying pastor gets direction through prayer, not the latest seminar.

I was deeply convicted by this realization. When I got home from that conference, I wrote letters to all the churches I had pastored, as well as to my former district superintendent. I asked them to forgive me for being a "pastor who prayed," but not a "praying pastor."

Confessions of a Senseless Shepherd

The words of Jer. 10:21 hit me powerfully during that time. "The shepherds are senseless and do not inquire of the Lord; so they do not prosper and all their flock is scattered." I began to understand more deeply that being a praying pastor would mean spending time nurturing and deepening my relationship with God. It would mean learning how to listen for His voice and His direction.

Jeremiah 23:18 describes this kind of relationship. In chapter 23, God was challenging the false prophets who were speaking "visions from their own minds, not from the mouth of the Lord." In verse 18, He describes a true prophet by asking a question: "But which of them has stood in the council of the LORD to see or to hear his word? Who has listened and heard his word?" The word from which "stood" is translated means to tarry, to dwell, or to stand firm. The words "council of the LORD" imply a close deliberation or intimate consultation. The word "see" indicates discernment or experience, and the words "hear" and "listen" indicate hearing with intelligence, and then obeying—even telling others. The implications for me as a pastor were clear. I needed to know how to hear from God, by spending time tarrying in His presence, in intimate consultation with Him, until I knew what He was saying, obeyed it myself, and told others.

Becoming a Praying Pastor

How do we get from being a pastor who prays to being a praying pastor? I offer the following suggestions, gleaned from my own journey:

1. Ask God to search your heart and reveal what is the true state of your own prayer life. Have you relegated prayer to simply an "option" among tools from which you can choose? Or is it the basis for direction and decision-making in your life and ministry?

2. Ask the Lord to lead you into a deeper prayer life with Him. This means deepening your relationship with Him. Have you been skimming along, allowing sermon preparation to suffice for your "in the Word time"? Or are you feeding your soul and seeking God above all other things?

3. Develop your ability to discern and hear the voice of the Lord. All through God's history with man, God has spoken to His people. Through the Word, and through the Spirit of God who dwells within you, listen for and learn how to recognize His voice.

4. Seek out the intercessors in your church and ask them to pray for you about this. You might be surprised how delighted they would be to pray for you to become a "praying pastor."

God is calling His people—and His pastors—to know the power and privilege of prayer. From Jim Cymbala (*Fresh Wind, Fresh Fire*) to Henry Blackaby (*Experiencing God*), the word is the same: Prayer must be our first resource, not our last resort.

Lord, help those You have called as pastors to be people who know how to pray first. Robert Murray McCheyne once said, "Study universal holiness of life. Your whole usefulness depends on this, for your sermons last but an hour or two; your life preaches all the week. If Satan can only make a covetous minister, a lover of praise, of pleasure, of good eating, he has ruined your ministry. Give yourself to prayer and get your texts, your thoughts, and your words from God. Martin Luther spent his best three hours in prayer."

The Pastor as Prayer Leader

By Jonathan Graf

Jesus said, "My house will be called a house of prayer" (Mt. 21:13). While Jesus may have intended something even broader in this statement, I believe that at least part of His intent was this: in a gathering of believers that is truly a "house of prayer," prayer will be the core value in everything that is done. Our goal for this book is to articulate what that might mean in a church, and to offer some practical suggestions on how to move your own church toward becoming a house of prayer.

The book is directed mainly toward the prayer leader, a lay or staff person who comes alongside the pastor to administer and organize prayer. The articles haven't focused as much on what the senior pastor can do. The pastor's role, however, is critical, and I want to offer some insights here. My suggestions are based upon what I've seen in churches that are on the journey toward becoming houses of prayer, and those that are not moving at all.

Preaching on Prayer

My first observation: Churches that are growing in prayer are churches in which pastors are preaching on prayer. Their people are hearing about prayer, and not just seeing an announcement in the bulletin or hearing an announcement about a prayer meeting.

Churches that are growing in prayer are churches whose attendees regularly receive instruction, challenge, and encouragement on prayer from the pulpit. Years don't go by between sermons on prayer, but only weeks. The congregation assumes the centrality of prayer because it hears so much about it from the pastor.

Dee Duke, the pastor of one of the praying-est churches I know, Jefferson Baptist in Jefferson, Oregon, preaches on prayer at least 13 times a year. That's one quarter of the Sundays! A huge percentage of the church's people are involved in prayer ministries. They live its importance.

Recently I spoke at Rainbow Acres Church of God in Indianapolis, Indiana. This church is growing in its prayer intensity. I was impressed by how many people (in a congregation of about 250) are involved in its prayer ministries. The reason, according to its prayer leader, is that Pastor Tom Whitesel preaches on prayer, or emphasizes prayer in his sermons, at least twice a month!

How can people not be moved to pray when they hear about it so often? Pastor, how often are you preaching on prayer?

Modeling Prayer

My second observation: Churches that are growing in prayer have pastors who model prayer. By that I do not mean that you have to go to or lead every prayer gathering in your church. You certainly should attend the ones you can, and even lead enough of them to model for your congregation that you view prayer as important. But modeling prayer also means that you use illustrations from your own prayer life, you highlight testimonies of answered prayer in the life of your congregation, you work hard to incorporate creative prayer opportunities in the worship service, you regularly pray in front of them (beyond the Pastoral Prayer), and you pray for the congregation.

Pastor, I am not trying to put yet another heavy burden on your shoulders. Rather, I'm trying to take one off—because you'll find that the more you encourage prayer in your people, the more God will work. And the more God works, the less you will have to strive. Lead the way through prayer.

CHAPTER SIX

What Does Scripture Say?

A Bible Study for Church Leadership

By Sandra Higley

*J*esus Christ intended for His church to be a praying church—a house of prayer. The first century church caught the vision and operated in that capacity, but somewhere along the line, the vision was lost.

After reading through this book, perhaps you and the leadership of your church should consider what Scripture says about prayer and the church. Here are some verses for you and your leadership to contemplate. Let this be a springboard to deeper study. Hopefully, revisiting the priority given to prayer by Jesus and the early church will help realign thinking with His standard and provide motivation to make changes where needed.

1. What kind of personal example did Jesus set for His followers through His own prayer life? (Mt. 14:23, 26:38-39; Mk. 1:35, 6:46; Lk. 3:21-22, 6:12, 9:18, 11:1; Jn. 6:15) _____

_____

_____

_____

2. What priority did Jesus give to instruction on prayer? (Mt. 5:44, 6:5-8, 9:38, 18:19, 21:21-22; Mk. 9:29, 11:17, 14:38; Lk. 11:1-13, 22:40)

_____

_____

_____

_____

_____

_____

_____

3. How did Jesus understand His own need in regard to prayer? (Jn. 5:19-20, 7:16, 8:28, 38, 12:49, 15:15, 17:7) _____

_____

_____

_____

_____

_____

_____

4. Jesus commissioned His disciples to spread the gospel throughout the earth—but what were they to do before they made any move toward fulfilling that command? (Acts 1:4-5,12-14; 2:1 [KJV])

_____

_____

_____

_____

_____

5. As the early church met together, four aspects of ministry were given equal importance (Acts 2:42). List them:

(1) _____

(2) _____

(3) _____

(4) _____

What were the results? (Acts 2:43-47) _____

_____

_____

_____

_____

_____

6. What evidence is there that the early church maintained its participation in corporate prayer? (Acts 4:24, 12:1-17, 16:13, 21:5) _____

_____

_____

_____

_____

_____

7. What can we learn about the importance of prayer as taught to the early church? (Eph. 6:18; 1 Thess. 5:17; 1 Tim. 2:1-8; Jas. 4:2b, 5:13-15)

_____

_____

_____

_____

_____

8. What steps did the church leaders take to preserve their prayer times? (Acts 6:1-4) _____

_____

_____

_____

_____

_____

9. What does this tell us about the importance they placed on prayer?

_____

_____

_____

_____

_____

_____

10. How does this compare to the emphasis your own church places on prayer? Corporately? As individuals? _____

_____

_____

_____

_____

_____

What action steps could you take to reprioritize prayer in your church? If you are already a praying church, how can you go deeper?

_____

_____

_____

_____

_____

About the Authors and Compilers

DAVID BUTTS is the director of the Denominational Prayer Leaders Network, the founder and president of Harvest Prayer Ministries, and the facilitator of Harvest Prayer Network, an association of prayer leaders in the Christian Church.

DIAN GINTER, who went to be with the Lord in 1998, was a prayer leader with Campus Crusade for Christ. She wrote many of the prayer materials produced for its Great Commission Prayer Crusade.

JONATHAN GRAF is the editor of *Pray!* magazine.

FRED HARTLEY is the senior pastor of Lilburn Alliance Church in Lilburn, Georgia, and the co-director of the Prayer Mobilization Team of the Christian and Missionary Alliance denomination.

SANDRA HIGLEY is the editorial assistant of *Pray!* magazine.

LANI HINKLE is the associate editor of *Pray!* magazine.

GARY KINNAMAN is the senior pastor of Word of Grace Church in Mesa, Arizona.

STEVE LOOPSTA is the executive director of Prayer Transformation Ministries in Minneapolis, Minnesota. Previous to that, he spent many years as a local church pastor.

GLEN MARTIN is senior pastor of Community Baptist Church in Manhattan Beach, California, and a seminar leader for the Church Growth Institute.

CHERYL SACKS is a local church prayer leader, and the director of The Greater Phoenix Local Church Prayer Leaders Network, a network of prayer leaders who are coming alongside their pastors to mobilize prayer in their local churches. Cheryl also assists other communities in establishing similar networks.

TERRY TEYKL is the president of Renewal Ministries and the author of numerous books for local church prayer leaders. For more information, contact Prayer Point Press at (888) 656-6067 or www.prayerpointpress.com.

WESLEY TULLIS serves as pastor of prayer at New Life Church in Colorado Springs, Colorado, and as the director of the National Association of Local Church Prayer Leaders.

MELL WINGER is the national director of church relations for the National Association of Local Church Prayer Leaders in Colorado Springs, Colorado.

What Is NALCPL?

The **National Association of Local Church Prayer Leaders** (NAL-CPL) is a strategic network created to serve the local church prayer leader. Its mission is to empower local church prayer leaders to initiate, strengthen, and expand the prayer ministries in their congregations. To be a member, you must be approved by the senior pastor of your church. The membership fee is $75 per year.

NALCPL also sponsors a major conference for prayer leaders and pastors each year. For more information on NALCPL or its conferences, visit the NALCPL website at www.nalcpl.net. This is a one-stop shop for resources, speakers, trainers, seminars, regional conferences, etc., that can be geared to your specific needs as a local church.

NALCPL is a ministry of the World Prayer Center and the National Association of Evangelicals, in association with Mission America and *Pray!* magazine.

You can contact the NALCPL office at:

National Association of Local
  Church Prayer Leaders
11005 State Hwy. 83 North
Colorado Springs, CO 80921
Phone: (719) 268-8210
E-mail: NALCPL@cswpc.net
Website: www.nalcpl.net

What Is Pray!?

Pray!, a magazine designed to encourage a passion for Christ through prayer, was launched in the spring of 1997. Each issue of *Pray!* has a theme, general articles of encouragement that cover a wide range of the aspects of prayer, a news section on what God is doing around the world as a result of prayer, regular columns on revival, prayers of the Bible, and classics on prayer, and a section loaded with ideas to enhance personal prayer and the prayer life of a church.

Since it launched, however, *Pray!* has become much more than simply a bi-monthly magazine. *Pray!* has spun off *Pray!* Books, *Pray*Kids!, two websites, a number of products to encourage kingdom-focused prayer, and a seminar/conference/consulting ministry available to local churches.

Pray! Books is a line of books that provides practical help to encourage increased prayer in the local church. Go to www.praymag.com for information.

PrayKids! is a bi-monthly publication on prayer for 8- to 12-year-olds. It is available to churches in packs of 10. Individual copies are available as a section in *Pray!*. Go to www.praykids.com for information.

Pray! Prayer Guides is a line of bookmarks that include prayer points based on scriptures covering various topics (praying for your kids, your pastor, yourself, schools, etc.). Go to www.praymag.com for information.

Pray! also assists churches in encouraging prayer through the **speaking ministry** of its editor, Jonathan Graf. He is available to speak at weekend retreats, conferences, church services, and your church's or community's prayer events. He also consults with churches that desire to increase their level of prayer.

For infomation on any of these ministries contact:

Pray! • P.O. Box 35004 • Colorado Springs, CO 80935
www.praymag.com